Walks with Children
in the
Yorkshire Dales

Wharfedale

Walks with Children

in
WHARFEDALE

Terry Marsh

A QUESTA Guide

ISBN 1 898808 12 0

PUBLISHER'S NOTE
It is the responsibility of parents when out walking with children to supervise them and to make judgements about whether any part of a walk is unsuitable for them.

Readers are advised that while the author has made every effort to ensure the accuracy of this guidebook, changes can occur which may affect the contents. The Publishers would welcome notes of any changes you find.

Neither the author nor Questa Publishing Limited can accept responsibility for any injuries or damage that may occur while following the routes in this book.

Maps:
The maps accompanying the walks in this book are purely diagrammatic, and, with permission, are based on maps produced by Harvey Maps.
© Harvey Maps 1995

AUTHOR'S NOTE
Most of the walks in the book involve some measure of ascent, often over rugged terrain; the distances too tend to be a little longer than other walks in this series. Some very young children may find them tiring, but children of all ages have been seen happily undertaking these walks. But, it is for the parent to decide what is appropriate for their child.

Published by
Questa Publishing Ltd., PO Box 520, Bamber Bridge, Preston, Lancashire PR5 8LF
and printed by
Carnmor Print, 95/97 London Road, Preston, Lancashire PR1 4BA

CONTENTS

Explanatory Notes.. 6
Introduction... 8

Walk 1:   Bolton Abbey – Bolton Bridge............ 10
Walk 2:   The Strid Woodlands............................ 12
Walk 3:   Beamsley Beacon................................. 15
Walk 4:   The Valley of Desolation and
            Simon's Seat...................................... 18
Walk 5:   Barden Moor Reservoirs...................... 21
Walk 6:   Trollers Gill....................................... 24
Walk 7:   Barben Beck Round............................. 27
Walk 8:   Loup Scar and Thorpe......................... 30
Walk 9:   Linton and Threshfield........................ 32
Walk 10:   Grass Wood....................................... 35
Walk 11:   Kelber and Lea Green.......................... 38
Walk 12:   Conistone Pie.................................... 41
Walk 13:   Capplestone Gate............................... 43
Walk 14:   Great Whernside................................. 46
Walk 15:   Top Mere Road and Starbotton........ 48
Walk 16:   Dowber Gill....................................... 51
Walk 17:   Buckden Pike..................................... 53
Walk 18:   Cray and Scar House........................... 56
Walk 19:   Hubberholme and Yockenthwaite...... 59
Walk 20:   Along the Wharfe............................... 62

EXPLANATORY NOTES

INTRODUCTION

Questa Walks with Children are intended to introduce young people to hill and country walking. Across the series, they range from short, simple river or lakeside ambles, to fairly energetic ascents of fells, sometimes to a considerable height. The walks are not graded, but are intended for groups, with supervised children roughly between the ages of six and fifteen.

Only parents, of course, know just how energetic, determined and resilient their own children are, and so each of the walks gives no more than an indication of the distance to be walked, and the amount of ascent, not necessarily all in one go, you can expect to face. All of the chosen walks have been done with children, and children of all ages have been seen happily plodding along them – they do have remarkable tenacity and boundless energy at times.

But these walks aim to do more than give route descriptions. They aim to educate young and old alike in the interests of the countryside, and the history that surrounds it. So, with most walks a few brief notes tell you what you might find along the way.

MAPS: Simple diagrammatic maps accompany each route description. The maps are to scale 1:25000 (2½ in to 1 mile~4 cm to 1 km). They should prove adequate, in good weather conditions, to guide you round the walks, but you are advised always to carry a more detailed and extensive map of the area, such as the OS Outdoor Leisure Map for the Yorkshire Dales (Sheet 10).

FOOTPATHS: Almost all the walks are on public rights of way, permissive paths, or routes which have been used over a period of many years by custom and practice, but any mention of a path does not imply that a right of way exists.

It is unlikely, however, that you will be prevented from following any of the walks mentioned in this book, but you are asked to stick to the paths at all times, especially where they are waymarked, or go through or near farmyards, to be sensitive to the work of the dale farmers, particularly at lambing time, and to keep any dogs you may have with you, under strict and close control at all times.

EQUIPMENT: It is important to go well-equipped into the Dales, and for everyone this means adequate footwear and waterproof clothing. Small and growing feet will benefit all the more if footwear more substantial than wellington boots or trainers are worn, and will reduce the risk of slipping.

There are rough and wet patches on some of the walks, and for these you will find that modern walking boots with a cleated rubber sole are the best footwear. This remains true even during dry spells in summer: trainers, for example, offer no support to ankles, and while they might be adequate for walking along streets, they cannot cope with steep grassy slopes.

The Dales, alas, are frequently wet, and a good waterproof should always be carried, along with an extra pullover, cardigan or jacket to compensate for the lower temperatures you will experience as you climb higher.

Warm trousers, not jeans (which are useless when wet, and offer no protection), are advised, though you don't need expensive walking breeches. Carry extra food and drink, along with your waterproofs and spare clothing, in a small rucsac. And always carry a compass, and understand how to use it properly.

ROUTE DIRECTIONS: All the walks start from convenient parking places, but do remember to secure your car against thieves.

The directions given in the text are usually right or left in the direction of travel. Sometimes compass directions, east, west, etc. are given. It is on the walks in this book that children can begin learning how to read maps and use a compass. Never let an opportunity to do so go by.

Distances and height gain are measured, and rounded up or down. Distances are 'Total Distance' for the round trip. Height gain is not always continuous, but reflects the many ups and downs you will face.

WHARFEDALE

Put simply, Wharfedale is consistently lovely, there is beauty at every turn, and spectacular stretches, as at Loup Scar, Linton Falls and the Strid. Through its midst, the river that gives the dale its name, gathers its crystal waters from hundreds of side streams, starting high on the moors above Cam Houses, not far from the watershed of Britain. But like all Dales rivers, it can change in a few moments from a sedately-flowing river to an angry, raging torrent, so that where you dangled your feet for coolness in the morning, you could be swept of them in the afternoon. That great historian Camden, in 1610, wrote: "Wherf runneth with a swift and speedy streame, making a great noise as hee goeth, as if he were froward, stubborne and angry."

It is not by chance that the splendid Dales Way follows the Wharfe in its early stages of its journey to Windermere, for here you find a perfect and irresistible blend of everything that makes up quintessential 'Dales' country. There is nothing unsightly, nothing to jar, nothing to cause you to take away other than the fondest memories, from the first easy walk around the Bolton Abbey Estate to the far flung upper reaches of Langstrothdale.

The scene that awaits is one in which the efforts of Nature combine with those of Man in a, for once, perfectly acceptable way.

The underlying rocks of limestone, capped with gritstone in a few places, are a perfect element for the many streams; the whole landscape has been formed by water, either free-flowing, or frozen in the form of long-retreated glaciers. It is a foundation on which Man has placed his imprint of winding roads, mines, walls, farm buildings and the most attractive villages imaginable.

By far the greatest part of Wharfedale is pastoral, and given extensively to sheep farming. The dale pastures sweep easily to the surrounding fells, and give way to upland moors where the call of the wild is borne constantly on the winds. And it is this combination of sheltered dale, gently-rising fellsides and rolling moors that make Wharfedale exquisite walking country. Anyone taking their first exploratory steps into the wonderful world of country walking could find no better place to start.

For the industrial archaeologist, the landscape abounds with the remains of the dale's former lead-mining era; for the historian, sites of very early occupation by man await. Botanists will be thrilled beyond belief by the inordinate richness of flora, while ornithologists, too, will find much to occupy their time. For that species of humanity that finds its pleasures squirming about in the darkness (and splendour) of underground caverns, the dale could not be better prescribed.

For years I have wandered the Dales, all of them, but I always return to Wharfedale, where so much lies in store. When I was called upon to write a guidebook to the Dales Way, the most perfect introduction to multi-day walking, I could not have been better pleased, for it meant a full and detailed exploration and study of Wharfedale. Dentdale and the cross-country routes into the Lake District provided some outstanding days, but Wharfedale was the scene of unashamed indulgence as I and my companions wandered backwards and forwards, always eager to experience again the charm of Wharfedale.

WALK 1:
BOLTON ABBEY – BOLTON BRIDGE

This is a brief, easy and relaxing walk on which to introduce young family members to country walking. The route simply follows the River Wharfe from Bolton Abbey, downstream as far as the old Bolton Bridge, and then returns along the opposite bank, a much quieter affair, since the right bank is shared by that delightful middle distance walk, the Dales Way, which starts in Ilkley and continues all the way to the shores of Windermere in the Lake District.
At the end of the walk there is opportunity to dangle hot feet in the river, or to explore the priory buildings.

Start: Bolton Abbey Estate Car Park. GR.071539. Charge.
Total distance: 3½km (2 miles).
Height gain: 25m (80 feet).
Difficulty: Easy walking, with a few unbridged streams to cross, and very muddy/wet in places.

THE WALK:

Leave the car park at the exit closest to the information kiosk and turn right to reach the village green. Take care crossing the road at this narrow point, and continue ahead to reach the Hole in the Wall.

Through the gate, beyond which Bolton Priory comes into view, descend a flight of broad steps, and as you approach the bottom, branch right across a sloping field and wander down to the riverbank.

It is well worth turning round and looking back to admire the splendid setting of the priory buildings, a most delightful location, to which you will return in due course.

Now simply follow the river in its direction of flow, but taking care to keep young children away from its banks. At times the river carries a considerable force of water, and must be kept at a safe distance.

The section of river along which you are walking, between Bolton Priory and Bolton Bridge, is just a taster of that delightful 80-mile walk, The Dales Way.

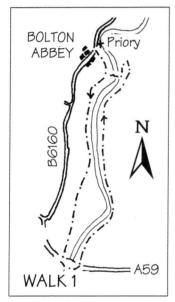

In a short while, the grassy path reaches the edge of Bolton Abbey cricket field, not far from the Devonshire Arms Country House Hotel. Continue along the obvious, green pathway to reach the A59 at Bolton Bridge.

This is now the 'old' Bolton Bridge, and carries the main road to Harrogate, usurped by a brash youngster a short distance away.

As you reach the old road, go left for a short distance until, just before the entrance of Red Lion Farm, you can go left (signposted) to a stile that gives access to a wide pasture beyond.

Keep directly ahead, aiming for the riverbank, and then climbing to a high viewpoint above the river, at a stile. Beyond the stile the path descends once more to the river, but is often very muddy and slippery, and, for a few moments, not at all pleasant.

But soon, you regain the riverbank, where you might enjoy a picnic lunch, or press on through a couple of field gates to reach Raven's Gill Dike.

A stile leads you on across the stream, then to climb slightly to a superb view of the priory and its grounds.

Continue following a fence (on your left) to a gate which allows you into the upper section of the wooded slopes above the Wharfe. A good path leads on, and down, doubling back to the left when it meets a lower path, and continuing to cross the Wharfe by a substantial bridge.

Once across the bridge, follow the obvious surfaced path back to the Hole in the Wall.

WALK 2:
THE STRID WOODLANDS

The Strid Woodlands are a superb habitat for wild birds
and a wide variety of animal and plant life. The presence
of the Wharfe, flowing through the woodland, only
enhances their appeal, and makes the woodlands a
remarkable place to visit at any time of the year.
The Strid itself is an amazing, rocky gorge, through which
the Wharfe rushes with fearsome force, and has claimed
many lives, of those without the good sense to keep a
safe distance away.

Start: Bolton Abbey Estate Car Park. GR.071539. Charge.
Total distance: 9½km (6 miles). The walk can be shortened,
by starting from the Cavendish Pavilion Car Park.
Height gain: Negligible.
Difficulty: Easy walking, but do heed the warnings
about The Strid gorge.

THE WALK:
As with the previous walk, leave
the car park, and head through
the Hole in the Wall. On this
occasion, keep ahead down the
steps, and on to cross the River
Wharfe by the bridge.

*Just upstream of the bridge
you can often see a line of
stepping stones, which would
have been the way across the
river in the days before the
bridge. In summer, when the*
*river is low, you can still find
daredevils trying to make it
across, with varying degrees of
confidence. It's good fun to
watch, but I don't recommend
you to try!*

Once across the bridge, go
left with the path and cross the
broad grassy expanse formed
by the river loop, and soon you
will enter delightful woodland
at a stile. Keep ahead all the
time, and you will eventually

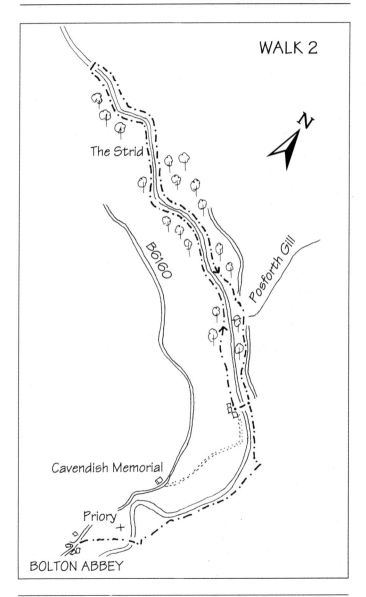

WALK 2

N

The Strid

B6160

Posforth Gill

Cavendish Memorial

Priory

BOLTON ABBEY

meet a minor road, Hazelwood Lane, near Pickles Beck.

Cross Pickles Beck by a ford, and turn immediately left on a footpath heading back towards the river, to a signposted path going right, through a gap stile, and on to a broad path leading to the bridge at Cavendish Pavilion.

Except during the winter months, you can get refreshments at Cavendish Pavilion, while the nearby Information Centre sells gifts, souvenirs, estate produce, maps, postcards and books.

Cross the bridge, and turn right, past the shop, to enter Strid Wood.

Having entered the wood, you are faced with a number of colour-coded walks (the pathways on which they are based were originally laid out by the vicar of Bolton in the 19th century, and you can obtain a leaflet about them all from the shop). All you need to do is keep going ahead, ignoring deviations, left or right, until you reach an information board close by The Strid.

You will need to divert a little to inspect The Strid gorge, but do take care not to go too close.

Continue following the on-going pathway, which climbs a little before returning to the river.

At a junction follow the path ahead, cross a neat arched bridge, and finally leave the woodland at a stile and gate.

Walk across grassy embankments to reach an old aqueduct spanning the river, by means of which you can cross to the opposite (true left) bank once more, where you take your leave of the Dales Way.

Turn right, and pursue an obvious pathway back into woodland that in spring and summer is alive with birdsong. You continue to follow the course of the river, but rather higher above it for much of the way, and wandering through splendid woodland.

Shortly after returning to river level, the path rises to meet a back lane, by means of which you cross Posforth Beck. A short way further on you return to the wooded confines of the river.

A good, clear path leads you out of the woodland, and on to an open meadow on the approach once more to the Cavendish bridge.

From the bridge (without crossing it), continue ahead to retrace your outward steps, to Bolton Priory and up to the Hole in the Wall, and the car park.

WALK 3:
BEAMSLEY BEACON

Beamsley Beacon is one of the chain of beacons used throughout England to warn of disasters or invasions. On it a bonfire would be lit, by its flames communicating with other beacons across the country.

The hill is more properly called Howber Hill, and its ascent is a popular outing, especially from Ilkley or Addingham. Here we approach it from Bolton Abbey, in order to visit the village of Storiths on the return journey.

The summit is, in spite of the hill's modest height, an outstanding viewpoint.

Start: Bolton Abbey Estate Car Park. GR.071539. Charge.
Total distance: 9½km (6 miles).
Height gain: 310m (1015 feet).
Difficulty: Easy walking, some on back roads.

THE WALK:

Leave the car park, and follow Walk 1 as far as Bolton Bridge.

Bolton Bridge is an ancient structure, although the new intruder was only built in 1993. There is mention of a bridge at this site as early as 1318, before which, and no doubt at times since, the Wharfe would be crossed by ferry. It is known that there was a bridge here in the 17th century, because it was washed away by flood water on the 17th September, 1673!

Go left across the bridge, and head along the road (the A59), soon turning right into Beamsley Lane.

When you reach Beamsley village, take the road to the left (signposted 'Langbar'), and follow it up the steep hill that follows.

As you near the top of the road, you will see a sign for Beamsley Beacon, directing you to follow a wall, to meet the main

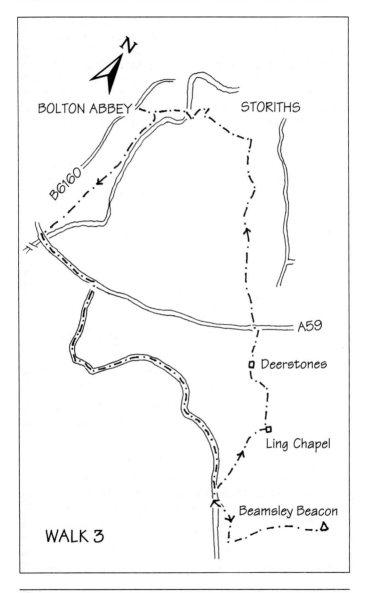

N

BOLTON ABBEY   STORITHS

B6160

A59

Deerstones

Ling Chapel

Beamsley Beacon

WALK 3

track across the hill.

Or, you can go further up the road and turn left between two houses on a signposted track leading to the beacon trig pillar.

To return, go back to the lane and down it to take a path, on the right, leading to Ling Chapel Farm. Keep on past the farm, cross Kex Beck by a footbridge, and walk on to Deerstones, from where an access road leads out to the A59.

Cross the road, go left a little, and then set off along the footpath to Storiths.

Keep following paths through fields to a stile at the lane below Storiths Crag. Stay on the lane, ahead, through Banks Farm, which then changes direction, and goes down to the top of the woodland above the Wharfe.

Follow a descending path down to the right, turning left at the bottom to reach the footbridge across the Wharfe, and then follow the broad path back to the Hole in the Wall, and your starting point.

BOLTON ABBEY ESTATE

The Bolton Abbey Estate is the Yorkshire base of the Duke and Duchess of Devonshire, and is a thriving, working environment. The Estate is open all year, and makes a valiant effort to combine the very special requirements of a unique landscape heritage with the interest that generates among visiting public.

The Estate focuses on the magnificent ruins of the 12th-century Augustinian Bolton Priory, part of which is still used for regular worship.

There is much to see and do on the Estate, from day-to-day work on the farms, the workshops, in the woodlands and high on the moors.

WALK 4:
THE VALLEY OF DESOLATION AND SIMON'S SEAT

In spite of a most off-putting name, this walk through the Valley of Desolation to Simon's Seat is the one walk in Wharfedale everyone should do. On this varied outing you will ascend through a deer park, where the last of the indigenous red deer of Wharfedale were held captive, climb beside attractive waterfalls, and through young woodland to a superb viewpoint, high on the heathered moors of Barden Fell.

Start: Cavendish Pavilion Car Park. GR.077552. Turn off the B6160 near the Cavendish Memorial fountain.
Total distance: 11km (7 miles).
Height gain: 380m (1245 feet).
Difficulty: Moderately demanding. Boots should be worn. No dogs allowed.

THE WALK:

From Cavendish Pavilion, cross the river, turn left into a field and follow the riverside path, which soon emerges from the trees, near Posforth Bridge. Turn sharp right, and walk back up the road for a short distance to Waterfall Cottage, and here leave the road by a gate leading to a clear track uphill. Aim half left, past a couple of venerable oak trees to a gate in a corner.

From the gate a path goes across to Posforth Gill, where a track leads down to the lower waterfall, a splendid fifty foot high cascade.

Although you can often cross the gill at this point if the water level is low enough, it is not recommended if there are young children in the party.

Retrace your steps to the original track, and continue to

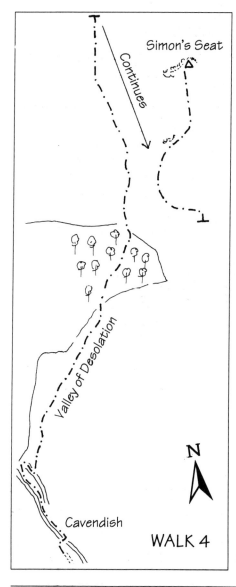

follow it through the Valley of Desolation to a footbridge, where you can cross the stream in comfort and dry shod.

The Valley of Desolation is so-named because of the devastation that was caused by a major landslip during a storm that occurred in the early 1800s.

Thankfully, Mother Nature, in her benevolent frame of mind, has seen to it that the worst of the damage is now concealed.

Now keep going along the north side of the stream to a fork, and here branch left to a stile into Laund Pasture Plantation.

Follow a good path through the trees to a gate giving on to the open moors.

The moors you are now entering are part of the Barden Fell and Barden

Moor Access Area. This means that although the moors are open for most of the year, they can (and are) closed during times when grouse shooting takes place (between August and December), or a time of high fire risk. Indeed, once you leave the road near Posforth Bridge, you are walking pathways that are permissive, not rights of way.

When you step on to the moors, you become subject to by-laws that are displayed at the access points, and which must be observed. All the by-laws are a sensible way of protecting the moorland heritage, and will cause little trouble for walkers. Dog owners, however, will find that dogs are not allowed on the moors at any time, with or without a lead, and the moors are regularly patrolled by wardens to ensure compliance with this by-law.

As you leave the plantation, so the path continues directly ahead, and leads clearly all the way to Simon's Seat. En route you will cross Great Agill Beck, at a ford, and go past a delightful stone table that is a splendid place for a picnic break. From here you can now see the top of Simon's Seat for the first time.

Higher up, the path crosses the feeder streams of Great Agill Beck and swings round below Truckle Crags, from where it is only a few more minutes to the rocky summit of Simon's Seat, and its trig pillar.

The summit view is quite surprising, extending into Skyreholme, a tributary dale of the Wharfe, to Appletreewick, and up the main dale to Burnsall.

To return simply retrace your steps, and enjoy a descent that is every bit as pleasurable as the ascent.

WALK 5:
BARDEN MOOR RESERVOIRS

Barden Moor has far more about it to justify your attention than at first might be supposed. As grouse moors, of course, they can be closed between August and December, or if there is any risk of fire, but at all other times you are free to visit them. If you do, you will find a landscape full of interest and variety. Gulls, coots and other water birds make liberal use of the reservoirs, while the moors themselves are covered in late summer and autumn with a glorious spread of purple heather that will gladden anyone's heart. In sheltered spots you will find rowan trees growing, while the moor sustains a scattering of bilberry and crowberry.

Start: Halton Height Car Park. GR.038556.
Total distance: 8km (5 miles).
Height gain: 130m (425 feet).
Difficulty: Moderate; a pleasant walk in spring and summer.

THE WALK:

From the car park take the tarmac track that runs down to Lower Barden Reservoir, turning left at a 'crossroads' to head for the in-flow of the reservoir.

Lower Barden Reservoir was brought into service in 1873, though it had been substantially ready for use for ten years by then. It formed part of a scheme devised in the mid-19th-century to supply Bradford with water, by linking a chain of five reservoirs from Grimwith.

From the in-flow you get a good idea of the complexities of reservoir construction, and cannot fail but to admire the ingenuity of the men who worked it all out in the first place.

Cross the in-flow by a footbridge, and join the main track

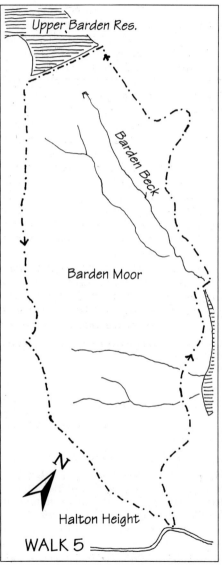

Upper Barden Res.

Barden Beck

Barden Moor

N

Halton Height

WALK 5

beyond that leads, left, to the Upper Reservoir.

You will often find black-headed gulls on the upper reservoir. Large numbers of these noisome birds breed here, usually in the less querulous company of mallards.

In winter, many of the gulls disperse, and are replaced by some of Britain's most fascinating species - goldeneye, Bewick and whooper swans, that swell the ranks of the more familiar grey lag geese.

Cross the embankment, to reach a path (signposted), back to Halton Height.

The route follows a causeway across a stretch of embryonic peat bog, and presses on to reach a bridleway, part of an important trans-country link in former times.

Each time, on your return journey, that you encounter

a junction, go left, and you will unerringly return to your starting point.

ALONG THE WAY: Heather: *You can find three types of heather on Barden Moor. The most common (Calluna vulgaris) is also known as ling. This is the heather that turns the moors to that magnificent purple from August onwards.*

You will also find bell heather (Erica cinerea), which favours dry ground, and should be distinguished from cross-leaved heather (Erica tetralix), which does not.

The heather is a natural habitat for red grouse, and you will almost certainly see or hear these beautiful game birds as you cross the moor.

From time to time, the heather is burned deliberately (but don't you try it!) and in a controlled manner, to encourage new growth for the grouse. For a while the scarred patches are unsightly, and the remaining branches of the heather grab at your ankles angrily. Thankfully, this walk involves no such close encounters.

But it isn't only red grouse that benefit from the heather. Moth larva, especially the northern eggar moth, love this terrain, as do the seven-spotted ladybird and the green hairstreak butterfly.

Many moorland birds put in an appearance - curlew, whinchat, wheatear, and golden plover, and their calls are an evocative reminder of the wild.

REPTILES

Barden Moor is the one known locality in Wharfedale of the common adder, a shy creature, rarely seen, that slips away as you approach. The slow worm, which is quite harmless, is becoming more common. It looks like a snake, but is in reality a legless lizard. One lizard, with legs, that you will find is the common lizard, often seen basking on drystone walls.

WALK 6:
TROLLERS GILL

This easy walk takes in delectable river scenery and explores the most fascinating limestone landscape in Wharfedale. It also visits the lair of a legendary hound of death, the Barguest, or 'Mauthe' dog. Appletreewick is reached from the main valley road, the B6160, at Barden Tower.

Start: Appletreewick. GR.053601. Limited parking.
Total distance: 9½km (6 miles).
Height gain: 160m (525 feet).
Difficulty: Moderate.

THE WALK:

From near the centre of Appletreewick take a path leading down to the river, through a field that in summer is used for parking. At the river turn left, keeping an eye open for river-based birds, especially the iridescent kingfisher. A short diversion over a stile on the left leads to a wooden staircase from the top of which you descend back to the company of the river.

Continue through another meadow and a pleasant stretch of woodland at the end of which, through a gate, you head left across a field to join a track out to a lane beside a bridge.

Cross the bridge and take a walled track rising on the left. Shortly, at a crossroads at Howgill turn left up Howgill Lane and go past the caravan site at Howgill Lodge.

Howgill is a scattered community at the base of Simon's Seat, and in 1310 was the site of one of the six hunting lodges that comprised the ancient Chase of Barden.

A short way further on, opposite an old milestone, turn left through a gateway, following a wall and switching sides of it. At another gate, aim for a stile beyond, then descending to

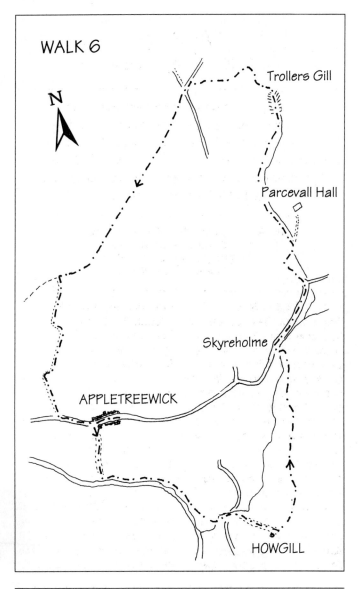

WALK 6

N

Trollers Gill

Parcevall Hall

Skyreholme

APPLETREEWICK

HOWGILL

cross a tiny stream beyond which yet another stile lurks.

Follow the line of the main stream, Fir Beck, on your left to a collapsed wall and footbridge. Cross the footbridge and climb to meet a lane, at Skyreholme.

Turn right, up the lane and continue until it forks, near a bridge. Here turn left to reach the entrance to Parceval Hall.

Parceval Hall was built in 1671, but has an Elizabethan look about it. It is generally regarded as the finest residential building in Wharfedale, surrounded by lovely gardens that are open to the public during the summer months.

Just before a wooden bridge go through a gate and follow Skyreholme Beck upstream passing a large grass-covered mound that once formed the dam of a large reservoir that served the Skyreholme paper mills.

Eventually, you reach a wall in front of the entrance to Trollers Gill, with the lump of Middle Hill on the left. Go right, to enter the gill.

Trollers Gill is a miniature gorge through the Great Scar limestone. Although more than 300m/yds long, the gill is narrow, dark and steep-sided, classic ingredients for monster-mongers. It is in the depths of Trollers Gill that you will find the lair of the Barguest, the spectral hound of Craven, a huge shaggy beast, yellow, with eyes as big as saucers. But, be warned, an encounter with the Barguest usually means death.

At the far end, where a wall descends to the gill, climb up to the left and over a stile across a fence, beyond which the way drops down to meet a path just above Gill Head Mine.

Unless you wish to visit the mine, now disused, turn right along its old access track, and when it swings sharply right, leave it, and keep straight ahead. Pass a small pot hole (Hell Hole: fenced), cross a stretch of ground that is invariably wet, and head for a wall, the road beyond being reached by a stile.

Go left to a gate on the right, signposted to Hartlington, beyond which a wide stony track leads out across the moor, level at first and then slowly descending, crossing two stiles en route. The track eventually becomes a green lane, and when, near a field corner, you meet a crosspath take the left path for Appletreewick. This is a winding track with excellent views of the many reef knolls that form the landscape along the North Craven Fault.

WALK 7:
BARBEN BECK ROUND

Between Appletreewick and Dibbles Bridge, Barben Beck fashions an attractive course through the Dales landscape. Above that, up to the massive dam of Grimwith Reservoir, the watercourse is the River Dibb, conceivably the shortest river in Yorkshire.
This walk rises to Dibbles Bridge from the delightful village of Burnsall over gentle hills, finishing with a peaceful stretch along the Wharfe.

Start: Burnsall. GR.032612.
Total distance: 9km (6 miles).
Height gain: 170m (555 feet).
Difficulty: Easy.

THE WALK:

Begin on the opposite side of Burnsall Bridge from the village, by taking steps down to the river. Go through a small gate, and then move away from the river to another small gate, beyond which you climb steeply to a gate at the top of a field.

Cross a back lane and head straight up the ensuing field to the top right corner and a stile. A brief encounter with another field brings you to another stile. In the field beyond, go half left to a stile giving on to another lane.

Head up the lane, but leave it at the first bend, at a stile.

Now follow a wall up the slopes of Langerton Hill, and after crossing the second cross-wall, go left along it to the top of the hill, on which there is a trig pillar.

In spite of its modest height, Langerton Hill is a fine viewpoint, and a perfect spot for a breather.

From the top of the hill head back to the main wall, either by retracing your steps alongside the cross-wall, or heading for a stile, which you can see.

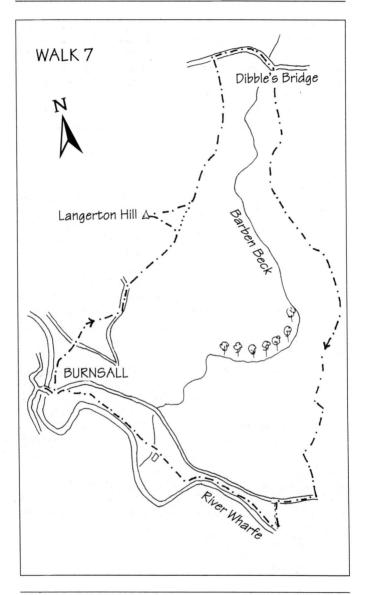

WALK 7

N

Dibble's Bridge

Langerton Hill △

Barben Beck

BURNSALL

River Wharfe

Cross the stile, and, keeping close to the on-going wall, descend a large field that slopes down to Barben Beck on your right.

At the end of the wall, cross a stile and head half right to another, in the angle of a wall, then follow a wall, on your right, continuing until you are near Turf Gate Farm. Look for a stile giving on to the farm access, and follow this out to the B6265 Pateley Bridge-Grassington road.

Turn right, and descend the road to Dibbles Bridge, soon after which cross a stile to reach an area of limestone. Cross this to the opposite corner, and go through a gate that appears directly ahead.

Keep ahead to another stile to enter a pasture sloping down to the beck. You cross a small stream, and then walk on pleasantly, high above Barben Beck.

When next you encounter a wall (collapsed) go left between walls, and cross a stile. Now follow the wall on your right, through a number of fields until you reach a gate at the bottom of a long, L-shaped field, beyond which a walled lane leads down to Appletreewick.

Turn right, towards Burnsall, and after passing Low Hall take an enclosed path leading down to the River Wharfe. You are now on the Dales Way, which will be followed back to Burnsall. The route is quite obvious, and a pleasurable way to conclude the walk.

Continue with the river until the pathways channel you through Woodhouse Farm. Keep straight ahead beyond the farm to a narrow footbridge, and on across a field.

As Burnsall finally appears ahead, you can make a beeline for the eastern edge of the bridge, beyond which the village is entered.

ALONG THE WAY:
Woodhouse: *This attractive 17th-century manor house was the home of an almost forgotten Wharfedale poet, John Atkinson Bland, regarded by some as the 'Wordsworth of Wharfedale'.*

Bland was a picturesque and kindly man, in his day the best-known man in the dale, and very much a champion of Wharfedale causes, whatever their significance. His letters to the press were invariably anonymous, leaving people guessing as to their origin, although there was usually a clue concealed in the text of them.

WALK 8:
LOUP SCAR AND THORPE

This short walk to the outlying hamlet of Thorpe hidden among green limestone reef knolls, begins along a dramatic stretch of the River Wharfe. It is one of the most beautiful walks in Wharfedale, and a perfect outing for young children.

Start: Burnsall. GR.032612.
Total distance: 7km (4½ miles).
Height gain: 90m (295 feet).
Difficulty: Easy.

THE WALK:

Begin by descending to the right of the Red Lion Inn on to a river path running behind attractive cottages and houses.

Immediately, the extravagant beauty of the Wharfe at its best becomes obvious, for every new twist in its trail brings a new view that is as delightful as the last. The river here finds its way through a narrow gorge, above which tall trees emphasise its depth.

The on-going path continues through a stretch of river known as Loup Scar, where the waters chuckle merrily.

A scene of beauty now, but in 1766 Loup Scar was the place where Tom Lee, a hot-tempered Grassington local tried to dispose of the body of Doctor Petty whom he had murdered. In the fullness of time, and after three trials, Lee was found guilty and hanged at the entrance to Grass Wood, where he had committed the crime.

The path to Loup Scar arrives eventually at a gate above the gorge, from where it descends to wander pleasantly amid woodland, to a suspension bridge spanning a stretch of river below Hebden village.

Do not cross the bridge, but take a path up the bank to the left, signposted to Thorpe. This leads to a quiet road through fields with an ever-improving view of the Wharfedale landscape. When you reach the road, cross it, and go along a small winding road directly opposite, *for producing shoes and slippers for the monks, the shoemakers travelling miles by packhorse around the Yorkshire landscape, cobbling their way*

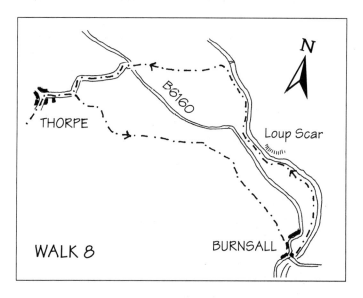

which will soon bring you to the concealed hamlet of Thorpe.

Thorpe lies hidden among reef knolls, a characteristic that more than likely saved it from the attention of marauding Scots in years gone by.

Also known as Thorpe-in-the-Hollow, the village is mainly a gathering of houses, cottages, a manor house and busy farms. When Fountains Abbey flourished Thorpe had a reputation

into the pages of history.

Retrace your steps a short distance, to the lower end of Thorpe, and back along the quiet lane until you reach a signposted lane for Burnsall, on the right.

Turn right along the walled lane. It leads through fields back to Burnsall, crossing Badger Lane and too-many-to-count stiles en route – though the arithmetic exercise will absorb young minds for the remaining journey.

WALK 9:
LINTON AND THRESHFIELD

This charming and easy walk visits the unique Linton Church, the village of Linton itself and the neighbouring community of Threshfield. The circuit ends at Linton Falls, the largest waterfall on the River Wharfe.

Along the way you will find examples of very early cultivation techniques in the form of 'lynchets', thought to date from the 13th century.

Start: Linton Falls Car Park. GR.001633. Charge.
Total distance: 5½km (3½ miles).
Height gain: 60m (195 feet).
Difficulty: An easy walk.

THE WALK:

Leave the car park and enter the church grounds.

Allow plenty of time to visit this delightful church, although you can return to it at the end of the walk.

Exit the churchyard at the far corner, by a path leading to stepping stones across the river, by means of which the ancient parishioners would cross to church. Don't use the stepping stones, but turn right, along the riverbank to cross a stile and climb behind a small woodland. Using squeeze stiles you cross the next two fields to reach the B6160.

Cross the road, and follow a signposted way up the ensuing field, passing two gates posts to a wooden gate.

On the way you get a good view of the lynchets in the adjoining fields. These are ancient cultivation terraces, constructed to improve the condition of the land so that farming was easier.

When you reach a quiet back lane, Thorpe Lane, turn right and walk along it for about 100m/yds to a step stile on the right, by means of which you can follow a signposted route down through the lynchets to a ladder stile, beyond which a cart track runs down to Linton village.

Linton Beck flows through the village green, and you can cross old lane round Linton House, and crosses fields to reach a humped footbridge over a disused railway line – part of the Yorkshire Dales Railway from

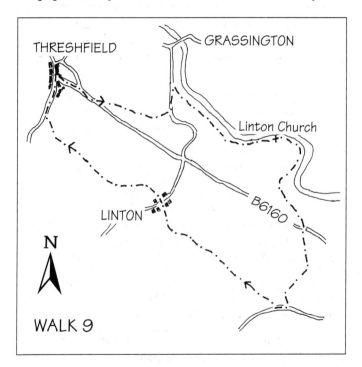

it by one of three different bridges – a clapper bridge, a packhorse bridge and a more modern road bridge.

Leave the village along the left bank of Linton Beck, heading for Threshfield. The on-going footpath leads down to an

Skipton to Grassington, completed in 1902.

Keep ahead from the foot-bridge, along a wall. Then, at the next field, head diagonally across to reach Threshfield, there turning right over Threshfield Bridge.

Go along the road opposite the Old Hall Inn to reach the B6160 again. Turn right for a short distance, and take the second path, signposted to Threshfield School. The path follows the line of a lynchet to another footbridge, also spanning the dismantled railway.

Turn left for 200m/yds, and then take the riverside path to Linton Falls.

Cross an in-flowing mill stream by Little Emily's Bridge, when a left turn brings you to the Wharfe and its magnificent falls.

Go on to the bridge across the Wharfe for an excellent view of the falls, and then go back and continue the short distance down the road to the car park.

ALONG THE WAY:

Linton Church: *The church dates from the 12th century, possibly built during the period of church building that characterised Henry II's reign (1154-89). It is of unique construction, squat and without a tower. The church was enlarged and altered at later dates, notably during the 14th century.*

Linton Church has served four parishes - Grassington, Hebden, Linton and Threshfield - and paths from those villages still run to the church.

Threshfield: *This village used to have a reputation for making 'besoms', i.e. brooms made from twigs of heather gathered from the surrounding moors.*

Linton Falls: *These outstanding falls are a fine spectacle and occur along the line of the Craven Fault. The present-day bridge is the fourth to occupy this strategic position. The first was known as the Tin Bridge, built in 1814 by the Birkbecks, owners of Linton Mill.*

This first bridge was covered with metal from old oil drums, across which clogged mill workers would clatter to work.

A second bridge replaced the original in 1860, and a third in 1904.

The present bridge, said to have a life expectancy of 150 years, was built in 1989.

Little Emily's Bridge: *is a small packhorse bridge on the original church path from Threshfield, and dates from the 14th century. It is thought to have been named after Emily Norton, whose family took refuge nearby at the time of the Civil War.*

WALK 10:
GRASS WOOD

Grass Wood lies only a short distance up-river from
Grassington, the main tourist centre of Wharfedale.
This delightful walk takes in a beautiful stretch of the
River Wharfe before entering the woodland, both habitats
proving firm favourites with birds and wild flowers, which
here are found in abundance.

Start: National Park Centre Car Park, Grassington. GR.002638.
Total distance: 7km (4½ miles).
Height gain: 130m (425 feet).
Difficulty: Easy.

THE WALK:

Leave the car park by a gate at the bottom corner to join Sedber Lane, a walled track leading down to the Wharfe at Linton Falls.

For a short distance, the walk follows the Dales Way up the right side (true left) of the river, signposted to Grass Wood.

Just after a wall, move slightly away from the river to reach an enclosed path below terraced houses, leading to the main road at Grassington Bridge.

At the bridge, cross the road and followed a signposted route to Grass Wood Lane, sticking close by the riverside as it rounds Ghaistrills Strid, once thought to be haunted, and enters the southernmost extremity of Grass Wood.

The path presses on through Lower Grass Wood to reach Grass Wood Lane. Turn left along the road until you can leave it, on the right, to enter Grass Wood itself, managed by the Yorkshire Wildlife Trust.

Shortly after entering the wood the path turns left and parallels the road until it reaches the edge of the wood. Here, turn right, and climb up the hill where the path bears to the right.

Continue on the narrow path, eventually leaving the wood and finding a way back to Grassington through fields and via Cove Lane.

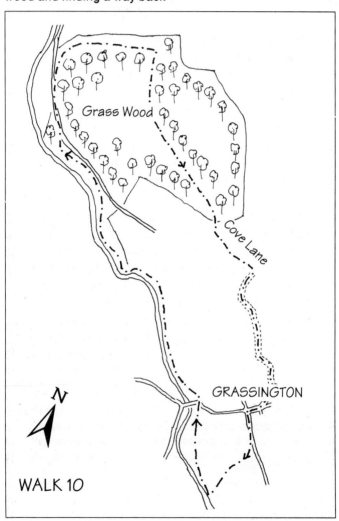

WALK 10

GRASSINGTON

Grassington has a fascinating history, and was already old at the time of the Domesday survey, having been an important settlement during Iron Age times. There are sites at Lea Green, and in Grass Wood, though the latter is rather overgrown. The town received its market charter in 1282, but developed during the 17th and 18th centuries on the strength of its lead mining on the moors to the north. The mines were worked by the Cliffords, the Earls of Cork and Burlington, and by the Dukes of Devonshire. Miners were brought from Derbyshire during the reign of James I (1603-1625). Ancient laws regulated the mining, under which those renting the ground paid a fifth of their product as a royalty. Many of the areas they rented were identified by stones inscribed with their initials, some of which can still be found on the moors. Early writers encouraged visitors to tour the mines, advising that "some of the shafts are reached by ladders and others by ropes."
– latter-day writers, do not!
Grassington Bridge, once known as Linton Bridge, was originally constructed in 1603 from wood, and then used by packhorses. Repairs and widening were carried out in 1661 and 1780, and the bridge raised to its present level in 1825.

WALK 11:
KELBER AND LEA GREEN

This fascinating walk takes you back in time, first visiting an area of field cultivation dating from the Romano-British period (100-300 AD), continuing on to the moors, passing the site of 17th- and 18th-century mines, before returning by way of the ancient settlement at Lea Green. In addition to its history, you can expect to find many beautiful wild flowers, and to encounter the rich birdlife in which these moors abound.
Choose a clear day!

Start: Grassington, National Park Centre Car Park. GR.002638.
Total distance: 12km (7½ miles).
Height gain: 225m (740 feet).
Difficulty: A high moorland walk, mostly on limestone (slippery when wet) and good trails. Not recommended in poor visibility.

THE WALK:
Leave the car park and head towards the village centre, go up Main Street, left along Chapel Street, and then right again, up Bank Lane, signposted to Bare House and Bycliffe Road.

At the end of Bank Lane turn right over a stile to find a long narrow pasture. Head for a squeeze stile at the top.

Height is soon gained on this walk, and already a fine view is opening up of the moors and the dale, with Grass Wood just below.

Follow the on-going path, and soon you reach a Celtic field system, almost 2000 years old.

This ancient field system is not instantly obvious, and best seen when the sun is at a low angle, as in winter, but look for a network of oblong fields, anything from 100m/yds by 20m/yds. Sometimes you can pick out the boundary walls and the ancient trackways.

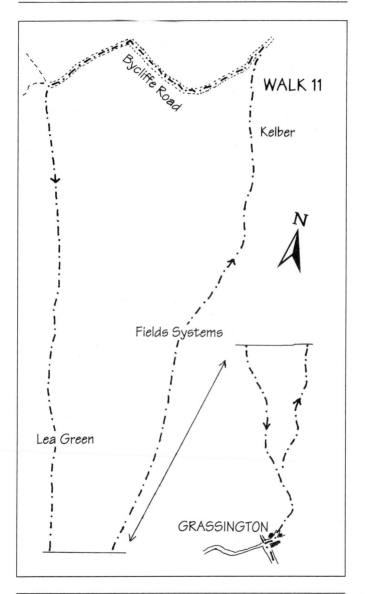

WALK 11

Bycliffe Road

Kelber

N

Fields Systems

Lea Green

GRASSINGTON

From the ruin of a former house aim for a footpath sign and stile ahead, beyond which you will find a ladder stile.

As you reach the ladder stile take the old track left of the signposted one, go past a walled dewpond (often dry), and leave the pasture at its top corner by a gated stile, soon to reach Bare House.

Bare House should more correctly be known as Barras House, from the Norse, meaning a hill farm. The first building on this site was constructed during the Viking period, while the present structure is a typical long house, with cattle and barn at one end and living quarters at the other, all under one roof. Very cosy!

Go round the farmhouse and past the corner of a wall, continuing up-dale on a well-defined track. Leave the track when you can reach a step stile in a wall on your right, across a field corner. A gate beyond leads on to a green lane across the brow of a hill, and through another gate.

Cross a ladder stile, passing a line of old mine shafts and then open hillside.

The remains of a wall ahead are a good place to look for fossils. You should find lots of 'crinoids', which were very small animals that lived in the warm seas of the Carboniferous period of earth's history.

A short way on, as you cross the area known as Kelber, you reach Bycliffe Road.

Turn left, down Bycliffe Road, it later becomes walled. At a gate continue ahead to reach a path crossroads near the top of Conistone Dib, a great, natural dry gorge.

As you walk down Bycliffe Road you encounter some fine stretches of limestone pavement, that might be worth peeping in to, to see what is growing inside the cracks.

Go left through a gate to cross the top of Conistone Dib, heading for a step stile.

You are now back on the Dales Way, and this will lead you all the way back to Grassington.

Along the way you pass some interesting lime kilns, more limestone pavement, the ancient settlement at Lea Green, where you should look for the remains of oblong huts within an enclosing wall, and yet more evidence of the mines that proliferate here.

You final approach to Grassington is along a narrow, walled green lane, bringing you back into the top end of the village.

WALK 12:
CONISTONE PIE

This brief walk takes you to an outstanding viewpoint overlooking Wharfedale and adjacent Littondale. There are far views up-dale to the swelling mass of Yockenthwaite Moor, and, closer, a good view of the field enclosure system of the dale.
Walkers wanting a rather longer version should look at Walk 13, which goes on to visit Capplestone Gate.

Start: Post Office, Conistone. GR.981675. But note, there is very limited parking in Conistone. Try just before the Wharfe bridge, or start from Kilnsey.
Total distance: 4km (2½ miles).
Height gain: 150m (490 feet).
Difficulty: Easy, uphill walking.

THE WALK:

Start down the road towards Kettlewell, but immediately leave it to turn right on a track through the wide green. Adjoining the last house you will find three gates; take the middle one and bear right.

On an improving path, climb into the dry valley of Conistone Dib, ascending through its narrow confines to emerge at a stile into a narrow field. Cross the field to another stile.

The Dib closes in higher up, but keep following a wall until a brief rocky bit takes you to the top.

Cross the wall by a stile, beyond which a short scramble takes you out into the open at last. Cross another stile, and turn left along a track – The Dales Way – to a gate.

Through the gate you reach an old packhorse route at the junction of Scot Gate Lane and Bycliffe Road.

Go straight ahead here to a signpost pointing out a green track running beneath a limestone escarpment, Hill Castles

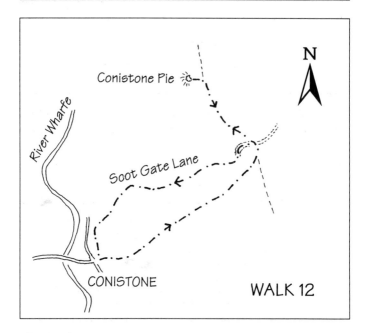

Conistone Pie

River Wharfe

Soot Gate Lane

N

CONISTONE

WALK 12

Scar, on the right,

Suddenly, ahead, the small rocky knoll of Conistone Pie springs into view. You can reach it easily by diverting left after the next stile.

Visible from many parts of the valley, this curious peak from a distance resembles a man-made tower. It is in fact a natural limestone sculpting, with enough nooks and crannies to evade all but the most determined winds. The view from it is especially pleasing, and well worth the effort of making this short ascent.

THE WAY BACK:
Go back over the stile and return to the junction of Scot Gate Lane and Bycliffe Road.

Turn right down Scot Gate Lane, and follow this ancient highway, tarmaced in its lower part, down Wassa Bank, back to the valley road, which you will reach only a few minutes north of Conistone.

WALK 13:
CAPPLESTONE GATE

This walk up to Capplestone Gate provides a wonderful
opportunity to inspect the limestone countryside of this
remarkable dale.
The walk is nowhere difficult, but should not be considered
in poor visibility, since part of the reason for the walk is
the outstanding view that awaits your arrival at the top.

Start: Post Office, Conistone. GR.981675.
Note the advice about parking in Walk 12.
Total distance: 11km (7 miles).
Height gain: 330m (1080 feet).
Difficulty: A moderate hill walk, rising almost continually to
Capplestone Gate. Not advised in poor visibility.

THE WALK:

Start from Conistone along the
lane towards Kettlewell, but
after a few minutes leave it for
Scot Gate Lane, an old drove
road, on the right, ascending
Wassa Bank. The lower section
of this ancient highway is
tarmac, but degenerates to a
rough track higher up.

As you reach the level of the
top of Conistone Dib – the dry
gully on your right explored in
Walk 12 – continue ahead to
pass a dewpond on your left
before entering the walled
Bycliffe Road.

*The area above Conistone
Dib is renowned for the quality
of its limestone pavement, and
is worth a few minutes of your
time to inspect it. Many rare
plants shelter in the vertical
cracks – grikes – which also
provide a foothold for a few
trees, a tough old ash or
gnarled hawthorn.*

Soon after passing through a
gate, Bycliffe Road – a rough
cart track – bends sharp right.
Leave the lane at this point by a
gate on the left, and follow the
signposted path beyond. It
passes two small plantations

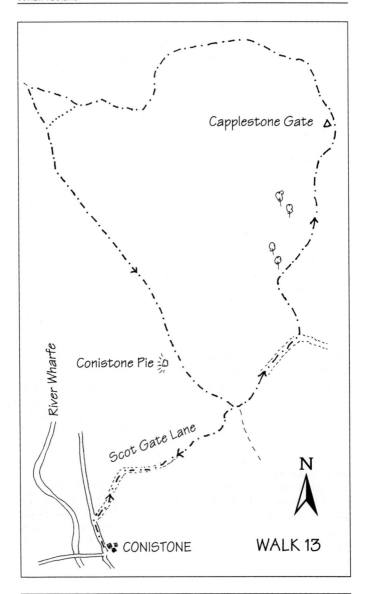

Capplestone Gate

River Wharfe

Conistone Pie

Scot Gate Lane

N

CONISTONE

WALK 13

and crosses a line of mine shafts. Now the gradient is rather easier as the trig pillar on Capplestone Gate comes into view.

Of particular interest as you approach the summit is the dramatic change in the under-lying rock structure. Lower down you passed through a limestone landscape, now you find the dark colours of millstone grit.

Capplestone Gate is an out-standing viewpoint. Great Whernside is the most obvious summit, being close at hand, but the distant view embraces Yockenthwaite Moor, Fountains Fell, Pen-y-Ghent and Pendle Hill.

THE WAY BACK:
From the trig pillar cross the stile by the nearby gate and turn left along a path close by a wall, passing through an area that has been extensively mined.

The spoil heaps are the product of the lead mining, and generally comprise what was regarded as rubbish – calcite, fluorite and barite.

You leave this upland plateau at a gate on the left, where the vastness of Wharfedale is suddenly presented before you. The descent is initially steep, but soon eases as it passes through a collapsed wall.

Continue downwards, the path forking at one point (either way will do), and rejoining not far above a gate in the lower wall.

Immediately through the gate, drop left, away from the main path (or keep on the main de-scending path a short way ahead), to join a level path lower down; this is the Dales Way. If you now follow it, left, through a succession of pastures and stiles, you reach the vicinity of Conistone Pie, which is easily reached from the path.

A short way on you reach the top of Scot Gate Lane once more, and can descend speedily to Conistone by your outward route.

ALONG THE WAY:
Fossils: *The rocks that com-prise much of this walk are well worth studying for fossils, including the fascinating lamp shell, one of the biggest you are likely to find.*

The areas of mining are also worth a moment of your time, though children should be kept under close supervision, especially in the vicinity of old mine shafts.

WALK 14:
GREAT WHERNSIDE

Great Whernside is the highest of the Wharfedale summits, a worthy and splendid objective from which to survey large tracts of the dale. Its summit is a vast plateau of rocks and boulders, beyond which lies the neglected Nidderdale.
This walk should not be attempted in poor visibility, when the summit proves to be a confusing mess of dark gritstone.

Start: Kettlewell. Car park near bridge. GR.969723.
Total distance: 8km (5 miles).
Height gain: 495m (1625 feet).
Difficulty: Quite an energetic mountain walk, on clear paths. Not advised in poor weather conditions.

THE WALK:
Leave the car park and head into the village. Cross the beck and turn right, in front of the Bluebell Hotel, which was established in the 17th century. Follow the course of the beck for a while, keeping on to a road junction near the post office.

Kettlewell, neatly-placed at the confluence of the Wharfe and a minor tributary, Cam Gill Beck, is a most delightful village, as one writer put it: "the peculiar abode of peace and quiet beauty...the limestone terraces, with the fringes of hazel and rowan coppices, give to the district a characteristic beauty."

At the road junction, keep ahead on the minor road to Leyburn, but soon, where the Leyburn road bends sharply left to tackle a steep hill climb, keep ahead again. Descend, right, past a former church, to cross the beck once more.

Over the beck turn immediately left on a broad track to a

signpost pointing the way to Hag Dike and Providence Pot.

The beck is Dowber Gill Beck, the source of which, up on the high slopes of Great Whernside, saw much lead-mining activity in the past.

Take the route to Hag Dike, ascending steadily above the ravine of Dowber Gill. The way is straightforward, waymarked with poles, and leads uneventfully to Hag Dike, formerly a farm house, and established in 1947 as a Scout hostel.

Between Hag Dike and the top of Great Whernside, the path you follow is not a right of way, but has been used by considerate walkers for many years.

Pass in front of and then all the way around Hag Dike to go through gates at the rear, from there ascending left up the rock-strewn hillside beyond.

A small relaxing of the gradient encourages a breather to gaze back down on the dale far below. The final slopes lead to the summit, which lies in the middle of a large group of millstone boulders, marked by a large cairn and trig pillar. The panorama is magnificent .

Go back the way you came, taking it slowly, the better to appreciate the beauty of the dale.

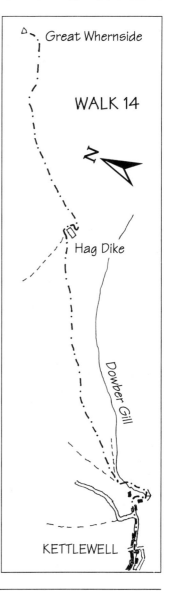

47

WALK 15:
TOP MERE ROAD AND STARBOTTON

This energetic walk leads first up an ancient road and then loses all the height to drop to the village of Starbotton. In complete contrast to the effort required to get up Top Mere Road, the concluding stages lead you quietly along the Dales Way, beside the Wharfe, back to Kettlewell.

Start: Kettlewell. Car park near bridge. GR.969723.
Total distance: 10km (6¼ miles).
Height gain: 325m (1065 feet).
Difficulty: Steep and energetic start, followed by easy walking. Good paths throughout.

THE WALK:

Leave the car park and walk left into the village. Cross the bridge in front of the Bluebell Hotel and turn right, following the road to a junction, near the post office.

Keep ahead at this junction, on the minor road to Leyburn, and shortly turn left to climb a steep gradient. Within a few minutes, when Leyburn road bends to the right, leave it for the easier gradient of a broad track between walls, signposted to Cam Head. This is

Top Mere Road, and its ascent is initially still quite demanding before it relents, rising arrow-straight up the tongue of ground between the Wharfe and Cam Gill.

When, eventually, you break free of the enclosing walls there comes an invigorating sense of openness.

The track soon meets another old path, Starbotton Cam Road, just before a small hummock. Go left here and follow the track as it descends, with splendid views over the dale below, to the

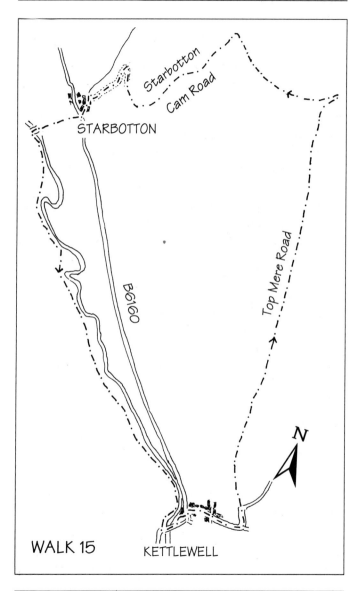

WALK 15

KETTLEWELL

STARBOTTON

Starbotton Cam Road

Top Mere Road

B6160

N

village of Starbotton.

Starbotton, halfway between Kettlewell and Buckden, is a compact assortment of 17th- and 18th-century houses, many a legacy of the lead-mining era. Today it is best remembered for the devastation it sustained on the 8th June 1686 when a terrible storm turned Cam Gill Beck behind the village into a raging torrent, pouring boulders and debris down the hillside and sweeping away or destroying many of the houses, most but recently built. The valley had long suffered the effects of flooding, but this was by far the worst.

As you come down into Starbotton go left through the streets and on to the main valley road, the B6160. At the southern end of the village you can cross the road, to follow a path going down to the Wharfe, which is crossed by a foot-bridge.

Once over the Wharfe, turn left, and follow the Dales Way along another admirable stretch back towards Kettlewell. This return route finishes by following the river as it bends, before leaving it by a path that climbs to the Kettlewell bridge, with the car park just beyond.

KETTLEWELL

This delightful, jumbled village cannot be much different today from how it was three or four hundred years ago. There is some uncertainty about its name, some authorities linking it with an Irish-Norse chieftain, Ketel. The village certainly pre-dates the Domesday Book, who surveyors visited this region in 1086, but they recorded little that might tell us what the community was then like.

Sheltered by high fells, Kettlewell, is a popular place at any time of the year.

WALK 16:
DOWBER GILL
AND PROVIDENCE POT

This easy walk into Dowber Gill provides a marked
contrast between a water-shaped valley,
characteristically V-shaped, and the evident U-shaped
form of the main valley, which was the
product of glaciation.
This side valley is a fascinating place, full of wild flowers,
and leads through a small area where lead-mining was
carried out to a popular pot hole.

Start: Kettlewell. Car park near bridge. GR.969723.
Total distance: 6km (3¾ miles).
Height gain: 260m (855 feet).
Difficulty: Easy walking on good paths throughout.
Most of the ascent can be avoided by returning from
Providence Pot rather than continuing to Hag Dike.

THE WALK:
Leave the Kettlewell and follow the route for Great Whernside (Walk 14) until, just across Dowber Gill Beck and the adjoining wall (Through-stile), the path divides. One way, to Hag Dike, is clearly signposted; the other goes right, beside the wall to a ladder stile, and on up Dowber Gill to Providence Pot.

Dowber Gill is truly fascinating, and will reward an unhur-ried approach. Here, for example, is a fairly rare occurrence of sandstone, the limestone can be inspected for fossil crinoids and brachiopods, and in summer, the spread of wild flowers is breathtaking.

Eventually this valley exploration will lead you to Providence Pot.

Entrance to the pot hole is covered by a concrete manhole, with a telephone wire in the

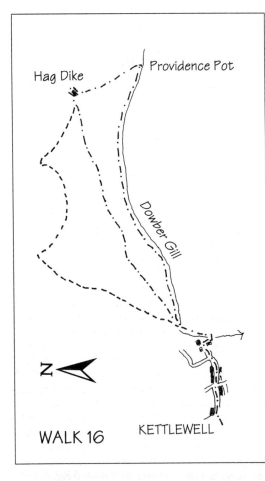

a few have had to be rescued.

From the Pot turn sharp left up a steep and well-used path to Hag Dike. [*Please note that this short stretch is not on a right of way. At certain times of the year you may be asked not to proceed, but as a rule sensible walkers are not prevented from walking up to Hag Dike.*]

From Hag Dike, take the access track through the gate, and either follow it down to the valley, there

stream bed. The wire is needed because this is a variant entrance into Dow Cave, one that is profoundly complicated. Its difficulties have perplexed many a would-be hopeful, and more than turning left along a walled lane to rejoin your outward route at Dowber Gill Beck, or, take a clear, waymarked path down the hillside above Dowber Gill to the same spot (this is the shorter).

WALK 17:
BUCKDEN PIKE

Buckden Pike is the second highest summit in Wharfedale, neatly placed behind the village of Buckden. Its ascent is a popular and uncomplicated walk, moderately demanding, and a 'conquest' that will appeal to children still in the early stages of their hill walking career.

Start: Buckden village car park. GR.942774.
Total distance: 7½km (4¾ miles).
Height gain: 460m (1510 feet).
Difficulty: Moderate uphill walk.

THE WALK:

The car park lies on the north side of Buckden village, and you leave it by a gate at its northern end. This gives access to a sloping track known as Buckden Rake, which climbs through the sparse trees of Rakes Wood. This is part of the Roman road over to Wensleydale, that ran from Ilkley to Bainbridge.

As you rise beyond the trees you get a good view of Hubberholme and the upper dale, known as Langstroth-dale. At a gate the track levels for a while, until you reach a second gate, at which you fork right, resuming the upward climb through a succession of gates and pastures.

From the top of the last field the path heads up the open hillside, but you are effectively contained by a wall, and directed straight to the summit.

The highest point on what is a fairly level summit, is marked by a trig pillar and a large cairn.

The summit of Buckden Pike is a fine place to have a picnic break. If it is crowded, cross the stile and walk directly away from the summit for a short distance, when you will come to the upper reaches of an

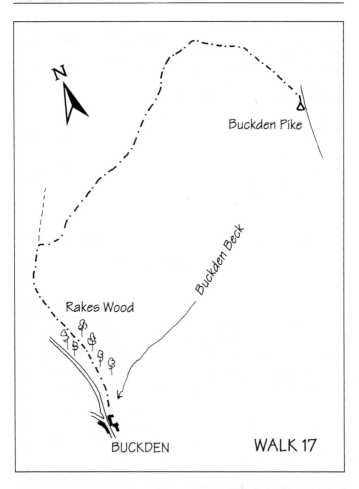

Buckden Pike

Buckden Beck

Rakes Wood

BUCKDEN

WALK 17

infrequently-visited dale, Walden.

The simplest return is back the way you came.

BUCKDEN: *Buckden is 'the* *valley of the bucks', a clear sign that deer once roamed here. Indeed, it was the home of deer as far back as records go, until the early 1950s.*

The settlement of Buckden

is a Norman foundation, set up as part of the medieval hunting forest of Longstrothe, and originally the creation of the Percys of Northumberland.

Years ago, Buckden was a bustling place, the 'last village in Wharfedale'. In those former times, when population movement took people from the dales to places like Lancashire, returning Dales-folk, coming home for holidays, could take a coach as far as Buckden from where they walked on across to Wensleydale and Swaledale.

The village used to boast three inns: the 'Low Cock', in a yard opposite Buckden House, was the first to go, while the white house up a lane at the top end of the village was formerly the 'High Cock'. Now only 'The Buck Inn' remains, and here farmers used to come to sell their wool.

WILD FLOWERS

One of the truly endearing features of all the Dales, and Wharfedale especially, is the magnificent wealth of wild flowers you will find. Of course, it is no use looking where sheep are to be found grazing, only low-lying and hardy flowers will survive their attentions. But the lime rich soils produce a host of flowers to gladden any botanists heart.

From March onwards you should start keeping your eyes open: lesser celandine, pink butterbur and coltsfoot are among the first to put in an appearance, closely followed by primroses and anemones, lady's smock and kingcups. Most, however, appear between mid-May and early July, and then it is that the hillsides, the moors and wooded slopes are bright with Nature's colour.

WALK 18:
CRAY AND SCAR HOUSE

Cray is perched bravely on the steeply descending highway from Aysgarth in Wensleydale, with a clutter of miniature waterfalls nearby.

Beyond Cray, a delightful walk, high above the dale, leads to Scar House, where the Quaker tradition flourished strongly in the 17th and 18th centuries.

This walk visits both places, before returning along a short stretch of the Dales Way.

Start: Buckden village car park. GR.942774.
Total distance: 8km (5 miles).
Height gain: 105m (345 feet).
Difficulty: Moderate.

THE WALK:

Leave the car park at its northern end, and start up the broad track that rises easily through Rakes Wood; this is the first stage of the ascent of Buckden Pike (Walk 17).

As a gate is approached the angle of the rake eases, and soon a track deviates uphill towards higher ground. Ignore this, it leads up to Buckden Pike, and continue ahead along the level edge of a limestone escarpment.

Soon you reach a wall and gate with a narrow stile to the right. Squeeze through the stile and keep ahead for a short distance to a narrow gate where a footpath sign indicates a descent to Cray, the tiny hamlet you can see below.

With the benefit of height, the whole of the limestone landscape is clearly seen, from the high moorland plateaux to the deep trough in which the juvenile Wharfe ambles sedately along.

From the gate the descent to Cray is initially steep and leads down beside a wall to a footpath

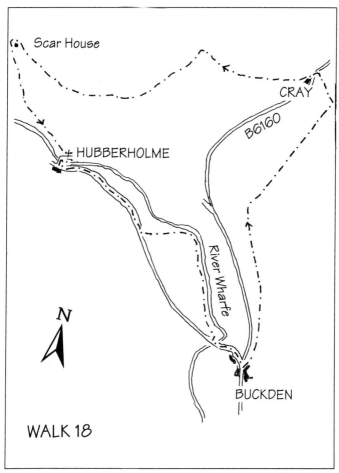

Scar House

CRAY

B6160

HUBBERHOLME

River Wharfe

N

BUCKDEN

WALK 18

sign, and a short descent to a gate. Just here Cray Gill is encountered, and crossed by a shallow ford, to reach the road.

The nearby White Lion Inn is a perfect excuse on a hot summer's day to take a break.

Continue behind the inn on a broad farm track, signposted to Stubbing Bridge and Yocken-thwaite. Two tracks are encountered, with the higher proving to be the better route, leading to a gate, where the onward route to Scar House is signposted.

From the gate the continuation is evident enough, and keeps to the edge of the escarpment, with only one slight deviation to cross Crook Gill by a bridge. Keep ahead along a level grassy ledge.

The on-going path closes in on a wall, and squeezes round its edge directly above Hubberholme, before continuing, less evenly, and trending right to keep above the intake wall, soon to reach Scar House, once a lively place of worship.

From Scar House you can descend directly to Hubberholme, there passing round the church, and over the Wharfe bridge to turn left along the road, heading back towards Buckden.

Before long you leave the road for a path on the left which loops alongside the Wharfe, safely away from the valley road, which is busy in summer.

Eventually, the path does return to the road not far from another bridge spanning the Wharfe, beyond which the village is only a short uphill stroll away.

SCAR HOUSE

It was at Scar House that there grew and flourished the new religion of the Quakers, largely inspired by George Fox, whose vision on Pendle Hill of "a great people in white raiment by a river side, coming to the Lord" sent him charging about these northern parts preaching the perfectibility of all men through inward personal experiences.

George Fox is known to have visited Scar House twice, in 1652 and 1677, though it is not certain that the remains of Scar House today are exactly the same as those he knew.

WALK 19:
HUBBERHOLME AND YOCKENTHWAITE

This short walk is an unashamed attempt to make the most of the delectable landscape that greets you at the entrance to Langstrothdale. It climbs from Hubberholme, a place of much interest, to Scar House, described in Walk 18, and then continues along the limestone escarpment to the farming community at Yockenthwaite, before retreating along a fine section of the Dales Way.

Start: Hubberholme church. GR.926783. Limited parking.
Total distance: 5km (3 miles).
Height gain: 120m (395 feet).
Difficulty: Uphill to start, but then easy.

THE WALK:

Go through a gate near the church, and once beyond the churchyard wall ignore a sign-posted path across meadow-land, and follow instead a wide access track leading up quite steadily to Scar House.

From Scar House go left and continue across limestone pavement to a gate and a gap stile in a wall. The on-going path, a delight to walk, continues along the southern edge of Yockenthwaite Moor, a bleak and forbidding place at the best of times.

The path eventually meets a broad access track above the hamlet of Yockenthwaite, and this is followed down to the valley.

Along the way you will pass, usually unnoticed, the entrance to Strans Gill Pot, a remarkable cave system that was only discovered as recently as 1967. It contains one of the finest decorated cave passages in the Pennines, though this can only be seen by the most experienced and slimmest of potholers!

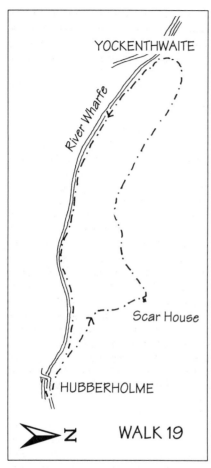

YOCKENTHWAITE

River Wharfe

Scar House

HUBBERHOLME

Z   WALK 19

The final point of access to the riverside Dales Way is via a narrow gap.

Once you are back on the riverbank, the way back to Hubberholme is a delight, simply following the river.

The Wharfe is a popular river with many birds that depend on its waters and the plants they sustain for their food. Dippers are frequent visitors, darting low above the water or bobbing about on water-lapped rocks, pied and grey wagtails are often seen, too. While in the flanking trees and meadows, and along the mossy walls look for tree creepers, nuthatches, wheatears, meadow pipits and many of the tit family of birds.

The path reaches Hubberholme on the Scar House access track behind the church.

At Yockenthwaite you meet again the Dales Way. To make your return journey, you need to go left through a number of muddy sheep enclosures – don't go down to the bridge.

ALONG THE WAY:
Hubberholme: *Recorded as "Huburgham" in the Domesday book, Hubberholme is noted as part of the manor of Kettlewell.*

The church, St Michael and

All Angels, is well worth a close inspection since it contains one of only two remaining rood lofts in Yorkshire.

Originally, the church was used as a forest chapel, and in 1241 given to the Monks of Coverham Abbey by William de Percy. It has always been an isolated church, indeed, in 1743, the Reverend Miles Wilson announced that his services at Hubberholme would be "once every Lord's Day in the afternoon, except in the winter quarter, when it is in the forenoon every other Sunday, because it is with great danger and difficulty I pass over very high mountains and large drifts of snow to the chapel."

The church contains a number of altars, and at one time the Parish Clerk, who was also the landlord of the George Inn opposite, took one of the altars for use as an ale bench, claiming that as Parish Clerk he was entitled to put the altar where he wanted.

On the first Monday in the New Year (except on New Year's Day itself) the George Inn is the scene for an annual land-letting ceremony, which takes the form of an auction timed by candlelight, at which bids are made for a year's use of a pasture owned by the church. The last bid before the flame flickers out becomes the rent payable. The rent from the successful bidder is used for charitable purposes in the parish.

Yockenthwaite: The name of this farming community has puzzled people for centuries, and is found in various forms in the parish registers. One parson actually wrote it as "Yoke and White". In 1241 it appeared as "Yoghannesthweit", from which you can glean something of its meaning. "Thwaite" is a word commonly used throughout northern Britain to mean a clearing, as in a forest, while "Yoghannes" seems to be a corruption of the Old Irish personal name, Eogan.

So, Yockenthwaite, is "Eogan's clearing", i.e. the land that Eogan used to farm.

WALK 20:
ALONG THE WHARFE

This is a linear walk, along the River Wharfe between
Buckden and Beckermonds, when you will see the river in
its most delightful reaches.
Taken in full, you will need cars at both ends of the walk,
but you can 'break manageable chunks off', and do smaller
sections – Hubberholme–Yockenthwaite, Yockenthwaite–
Beckermonds – piecemeal over a few days,
simply returning by the same route, without lessening
your enjoyment of the walk.

Start: Buckden village car park. GR.942774.
Total distance: 8½km (5¼ miles).
Height gain: 80m (260 feet).
Difficulty: Easy.

THE WALK:
The first objective is the hamlet of Hubberholme, reached by descending from the car park into the village and bearing right along a minor road leading to Wharfe Bridge.

Wharfe Bridge used to be known as Election Bridge two hundred years ago, a name derived from a speech by a would-be Member of Parliament in which he promised to have a new bridge built if the local people voted for him. He kept his promise, but only at the cost of essential repairs to Hubberholme Bridge, for which money had been allocated.

Just over the bridge take to a broad path on the right, signposted Dales Way, which follows the river for a while before finally returning to the road for a short stretch to Hubberholme.

Cross the bridge in Hubberholme and go through a gate just past the church. Once beyond the churchyard wall leave the wide access track to Scar

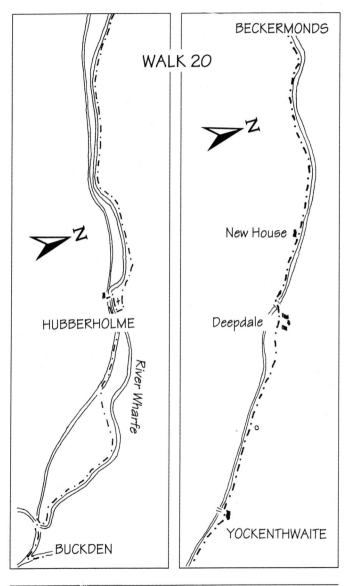

WALK 20

BECKERMONDS

New House

HUBBERHOLME

Deepdale

River Wharfe

BUCKDEN

YOCKENTHWAITE

House, and follow a lower path across pastureland, and so regain the riverbank.

The riverside path is never in doubt, and along it there are a few places where you can sit peacefully by the river for a while, but do keep an eye on young children, the Wharfe has strong currents and deep pools in places.

As you approach Yockenthwaite the path goes through a narrow gap in a wall near a gate. More gates and muddy conditions lie beyond before you reach a broad farm track. Go diagonally right and slightly uphill towards the main buildings, from where you can continue along an obvious track towards Deepdale. Near the farm buildings you will find a signposted path going left to a gate, beyond which the path eases along beside the river once more.

Not far beyond Yockenthwaite you encounter a prehistoric stone circle, once known locally as the Giant's Grave. This ancient monument is thought to date from the Bronze Age, and could be up to 3000 years old!

After passing the stone circle the onward path is less-pronounced, but it heads for a stile leading into an enclosed pasture where an indistinct path moves away from the river.

Go through a gap in a wall and on to a ladder stile to pass round the edge of a field before reaching a small footbridge across Deepdale Gill. A short way further on the access to Deepdale Farm is reached. Follow the track out to the valley road, and cross the river by Deepdale Bridge.

Over the bridge turn right to follow a wide path, between wall and river, later opening out as New House is passed. The way is unavoidably towards the far flung community of Beckermonds, rather larger than the earlier ones visited on this walk.

Just south of Beckermonds a footbridge spans Greenfield Beck, and a short, walled way leads up to the Beckermonds access road, and the end of the journey.

Beckermonds lies in a sheltered hollow on the edge of Greenfield Forest. It sits above the confluence of Oughtershaw and Greenfield Becks, which here combine to become the Wharfe, though the true source of the Wharfe lies higher still among the moorland slopes beyond.

This small community derives its name from the Danes, 'beckur' meaning stream, and 'mund' meaning mouth.